jennie Peskett

P9-DTA-342

creative ideas for teaching exceptional children

avaril wedemeyer · joyce cejka

Second Edition

Love Publishing Company

Denver, Colorado 80222

EDUCATION SERIES

Copyright © 1975 Love Publishing Company
All rights reserved
No part of this book may be reproduced in any form or by any means
without the written permission of the publisher.
Printed in the U.S.A.

ISBN 0-89108-046-5
Library of Congress Catalog Card Number 74-32611
10   9   8   7   6   5   4   3

CONTENTS

PREFACE 7

PART ONE / INTRODUCTION 11

PART TWO / Sensory Motor 17
Tracing Tray 18
Flashlight Trace 19
Mystery Box 20
Touch and Tell 21
Flip and Feel 22
Tracing Cards 23
Tie and Count 24
Button Board 25
Hand Shadows 26
Bottle Fun 27
Swing a Ring 28
Stringing Straw 29
Sequence Nuts and Bolts 30
Lacing Cards 31
Tong Pick-Up 32
Nail Lacing 33
Tile Patterns 34
Place a Pin 35
Gadget Manipulation 36
Roll a Line 37

Finger Golf 38

Finger Croquet 39

Sorting Containers 40

Color Match-Up 41

Color Concentration 42

Shape Hunt 43

Toothpick Forms 44

View Wheel 45

Add a Part 46

Which Way? 47

Describe and Duplicate 48

Felt Forms 49

Puzzle Pictures 50

Position Practice 51

Ditto Designs 52

Mystery Pictures 53

Right on Track 54

Grid Designs 55

Shake and Listen 56

Animal Jump 57

Turtle Hop 58

Line Obstacle Course 59

Variations, Sensory-Motor 60

PART THREE / LANGUAGE 65

Park and Stop 66

Quick Call 67

Alphabet Scratch 68

Sort the Stack 69

Seasonal Sort 70

Association Pictures 71

Sequence Cards 72

Absurd Pictures 73

Picture Hunt 74

Phonetic Dominoes 75

Space Fill-In 76

Add the Letter 77

Jumbled Words 78

Take a Look 79

Hang-Up Relay 80

Postal Sort 81

Check a Word 82

Compound Lotto 83
Deal the Deck 84
Reach Your Goal 85
Word Blender 86
Spelling Choice 87
Funny Sentence 88
Felt Fun 89
What to Wear When 90
Pop-Up 91
Motivational Assignments 92
Direction Drive 93
Team Talk 94
Three Little Words 95
Build Your Own 96
Move in Order 97
Quiz Cards 98
Variations, Language 99

PART FOUR / NUMBER CONCEPTS 103
Number Concept Cards 105
Step and Clap 106
Calendar Math 107
Drop a Line 108
Challenge 109
Button Dice 110
Make a Run 111
String Along 112
Math Bingo 113
Math Dominoes 114
Color by Number 115
Turn-Up 116
Count, Color, and Add 117
Dot Sequence 118
Add One More 119
Math Dice 120
Bowl a Number 121
Day By Day Bingo 122
Calendar Fun 123
Motivational Fill-Ins 124
Yardstick Race 125
Directional Bingo 126
Number Hang-Up 127

Place Value Dice--128
Measure Match --129
Variations, Number Concepts ---130

APPENDIX / CROSS-CLASSIFICATION OF
INSTRUCTIONAL ACTIVITIES ---133

PREFACE

This is a book of many people. We wish to express appreciation to our friends for their valuable assistance in the construction of this handbook.

We further acknowledge the children without whom this guide could not have been written. They made possible the laboratory in which this publication was inspired and brought to completion.

Avaril Wedemeyer
Joyce Cejka

PART ONE
INTRODUCTION

INTRODUCTION

The child who has faced learning problems and, as a result, has encountered frustration and failure often becomes resentful and rejects traditional teaching methods and materials. He may be afraid to attempt academic tasks due to past failure experiences or the fear of what new learning experiences may uncover. These conditions can cause the child continued unhappiness and frustration in the learning situation. It is not unusual for him to become a serious behavior problem in the classroom. Because of the child's previous learning experiences, motivation has to be a prime consideration. It is important to use materials and techniques that he is willing to accept. A unique format and learning game approach can help make school an enjoyable and successful experience for such a child.

Children with learning disabilities need individualized materials and techniques to increase their success responses. Feelings of success and achievement will aid the child in the way he approaches the next task. Self-confidence will be increased, and he is more likely to experience additional success. A more positive approach to a learning task can strengthen the child's performance.

TEACHER-MADE MATERIALS

Individualized educational planning, with materials specifically designed for each child, can result in an increase in his ability to learn and in positive modification of his behavior. Because there is a need for considerable review and reinforcement, many different techniques and materials must be used to present the same concept. It is often helpful to utilize a multisensory approach using a combination of the visual, auditory, tactile, and kinesthetic sense areas.

Although many fine commercial materials are available, they would be too difficult and time-consuming for an individual teacher to duplicate; but teacher-made materials can have an important place within a classroom. Materials can be designed for the development of specific skills or concepts. For example, a commercial phonics game might be unsuitable for some children because it presents eight sounds. A teacher-designed game might reduce the number of sounds to four or less or might emphasize those specific sounds a child finds troublesome. The format of a material might also be specifically designed. Some children may need materials without distracting elements, items of a larger size or fewer items on a card or sheet, color-cued items, etc.

Many of the materials suggested in this book involve separate cards for discrimination, categorizing, and association tasks. The child can manipulate the cards and actually place them together rather than point to matching elements or drawing lines between them. Motor tasks such as these also utilize the child's need for movement and incorporate it into a meaningful activity.

The items in this handbook can be produced at nominal cost, and the materials can be made according to a child's particular learning needs and within his ability range. Teacher aides and volunteers working within the classroom can help construct these individualized learning materials.

Although this publication is primarily designed for the teacher of children with learning disabilities, it may be of value for the classroom teacher involved in mainstreaming the mild to moderate learning disabled child. Many of the ideas can be incorporated into a regular primary-level program, but they can be adapted for programs for other age groups as well. The level of difficulty of the games and activities can be adjusted by varying such items as number of cards, number of items, the degree of difference among the items, the size of the items, or the amount of distraction within the material. Introducing the element of memory or a series of steps will increase the difficulty of a task. In selecting a learning game the teacher should consider the ability range of the child and either increase or decrease the degree of difficulty depending on the level of the activity.

These materials were developed while working directly with children who have learning problems. Variations and techniques emerged as the children's needs suggested change. When adapting these games, the following guidelines are suggested:

- Meet the needs of each child.
- Consider the child's experience and interest areas.
- Provide an activity within the child's ability.

- Use an attractive format—simple, colorful, motivational.
- Build from one game to another in sequenced concept development.
- Sequence games in degree of difficulty.
- Allow time for review in order to assure mastery.
- Allow the child to experience success often.
- Allow the child to lead in learning experiences.

PRACTICAL SUGGESTIONS

Items suggested in this publication can be made inexpensively, though with a reasonable amount of effort. Many items can be used interchangeably. Whenever possible, make standard card sets by using the same size cards. Card sets will be easier to file, store, or combine with other items. Use aides, student teachers, volunteers, scout troops, and even children within your class to help you construct some of the items. You will need to plan the materials in advance, but others could help with the cutting, pasting, and covering with contact paper.

The format of the items should be kept as simple as possible. Consider the size of the materials, the number of elements, and their placement on a card or game board. Make materials that are easy for children to handle.

Try to use materials that will shorten the preparation process. Materials such as gummed paper, velour paper, seals, mystic tape, and spray paint can speed preparation time. Small picture dictionaries, mail order catalogs, magazines, and old reading readiness, primary science, or primary arithmetic workbooks are a ready source of pictures for phonics, classification, and arithmetic activities.

Many materials can be obtained free of charge, such as fabric samples, cardboard from shirts or blouses, tiles, scrap lumber, film cans, and pill containers. Many useful items for construction of games can be purchased at nominal cost in a hardware store.

Making an item relatively permanent rather than expendable makes the effort more worthwhile. This may be more time consuming and often will add to the expense, but both time and money will be saved in the long run. If the materials are durable and have protective covering, the teacher will allow the children to use the materials more freely. Clear plastic spray gives a good protective covering. Many items can be covered with clear contact paper to prolong use. These have an added advantage—the children can mark on them with a grease pencil or a marking pen, then they can be wiped off and reused. Buy a number of plastic envelopes (approximately 9" x 12") for some of the game cards. Check with your school system to see if they will laminate materials for you.

It is important that materials are readily available to the teacher and the children. To facilitate this, an adequate storage system should be devised. Such things as shoe boxes divided into compartments, heavy duty envelopes, notebooks with celluloid covered pages, acetate overlays, clear plastic envelopes, and cards on rings will save space and provide for accessibility. A catalog file of each game will facilitate quick retrieval and greater use. Subject areas can be designated by different colored index cards—for example, language-yellow, arithmetic-green, etc.

ORGANIZATION OF INSTRUCTIONAL ACTIVITIES

This handbook is divided into three sections: sensory-motor, language, number concepts. The sensory-motor section includes activities in the areas of visual and auditory perception, tactile and kinesthetic skills, and both gross and fine motor coordination. Verbal expression, reading, and phonics activities are included in the language section. The section on number concepts includes a wide range of arithmetic skills ranging from counting and simple recognition of number groups to arithmetic computation and time, measurement, and directional concepts.

This handbook is not intended as a curriculum guide, but rather as a compilation of suggestions to aid the teacher in individualizing learning activities. The teacher must rely on her own resources to determine the needs of the child and to plan the curriculum content.

It is our intent that this publication will stimulate teachers to rely on their own creative resources and to use every opportunity for varied learning experiences. Children who enjoy a learning experience will find pleasure and success in their educational process.

We hope you will enjoy yourself and utilize your own creative resources and the ideas of your children to use and adapt the suggestions in this book. We are sure that once you have started you will think of additional ways to provide more opportunities for learning within your classroom.

PART TWO
SENSORY – MOTOR

SENSORY — MOTOR

Development of basic perceptual skills is essential to success in academic areas and other learning tasks. The sensory-motor section emphasizes visual, auditory, tactile, and kinesthetic perception. An attempt has been made to present the items according to the level of complexity and the major skill area involved. The general order of the items is as follows:

Tactile and kinesthetic activities

Eye-hand coordination

Directionality concepts

Position in space

Visual discrimination

Color and form discrimination

Visual memory

Body image

Part-whole relationships

Auditory discrimination

Gross motor activities

TRACING TRAY   Sensory-Motor

Tactile, Auditory, Visual Discrimination / Following Directions / Letter, Number, Shape Recognition

1. Fill a shallow tray or cookie sheet with damp sand or clay.

2. Following the teacher's directions and demonstration, the child draws forms with his finger or with a stick—for example, letters, numbers, shapes.

3. Prepared cards containing shapes can be given to the child to copy in the sand.

Note: To keep the clay or sand moist, store the entire tray in a large plastic bag.

FLASHLIGHT TRACE Sensory-Motor

Letter, Number Recognition / Number Formation

1. Prepare a series of large cards containing the letters of the alphabet. Use white cardboard and black marking pen, or black construction paper letters.

2. The child traces over the patterns, using a small flashlight in a dark room.

3. Prepare a series of line patterns. Demonstrate the strokes and have the child verbalize the directions.

4. Prepare additional card sets with numbers and shapes.

VARIATION: page 60

MYSTERY BOX   Sensory-Motor

Tactile, Color, Form Discrimination / Thinking Skills / Verbal Expression

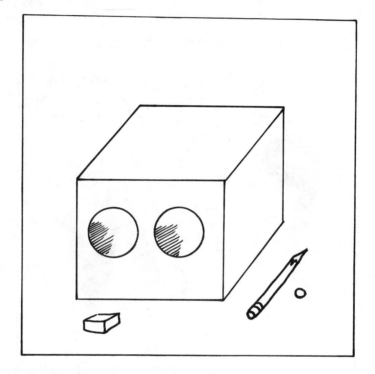

1. Cut two holes in the side of a medium-size box.
2. Put familiar objects in the box.
   a. Start with gross discrimination tasks—for example, objects of different kinds.
   b. Use other objects that can be identified by texture, shape, or size.
3. The child puts one or both hands in the box, feels an object, and identifies it.
4. Put two or more of the same object in the box. The child finds two alike.
5. Show the child an object. Direct him to find an identical or similar object in the box—for example, show one kind of ball, the child must find a similar kind of ball.

VARIATION: page 60

TOUCH AND TELL   Sensory-Motor

Tactile Discrimination / Word Recognition / Word Formation /
Word Matching / Verbal Expression

1. Staple or glue common objects to a 5″ x 8″ index card—for example, paperclip, toothbrush, button.

2. The child feels and describes the objects.

3. The child prints the name of each object on a 3″ x 5″ index card.

4. Once the child has printed the names of all the objects, he matches his cards with the object cards.

FLIP AND FEEL   Sensory-Motor

Tactile, Kinesthetic Discrimination / Number, Letter Recognition / Number Group Recognition

1. Cut numbers, letters, and shapes from sandpaper and mount on 5″ x 8″ index cards.

   a. Pipe cleaners, corrugated paper, or a braille punch can also be used to form numbers and letters.
   b. Shapes and simple outlines of objects can be prepared with these same materials.

2. Punch holes in cards and attach to metal rings for convenient use and easy storage.

3. The child traces the figures with his finger.

Note: Precut felt numbers/letters can be purchased inexpensively.

TRACING CARDS Sensory-Motor

Tactile, Kinesthetic Discrimination / Eye-Hand Coordination / Letter, Number, Shape Recognition / Number Group Recognition / Letter Formation / Reading

1. Attach a flap to the top of a tagboard sheet (see illustration).
2. On the flap, mount a picture that shows one item or object.
3. Print the beginning letter of the item at the top of the tagboard in upper and lower case letters.
4. Write a sentence, short poem, or appropriate tongue-twister on the tagboard sheet.
5. Fasten tracing paper to the tagboard with paper clips or cover with contact paper.
6. The child uses a marking pen to trace over the letters and words.
7. Use letters, numbers, and shapes for other tracing patterns.

VARIATION: page 60

TIE AND COUNT   Sensory-Motor

Tactile, Kinesthetic Discrimination / Counting / Number Sequence

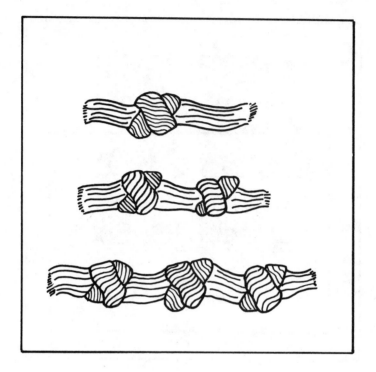

1. Cut a clothesline rope into several short and long pieces.

2. Make one or more knots in each length.

3. The child feels and counts the number of knots.

4. For finer discrimination, tie knots in string, yarn, or thread.

BUTTON BOARD

Sensory-Motor

Eye-Hand Coordination

1. Faster a large button at the center of a sturdy cardboard square or circle.

2. Staple loops of narrow elastic at intervals around the edge of the board.

3. The child stretches the loops and fastens each loop around the button.

4. Write a letter or number by each loop.

5. The child hooks a loop around the button as directed by the teacher—for example, "Put the 'A' loop around the button."

HAND SHADOWS   **Sensory-Motor**

Eye-Hand Coordination / Verbal Expression

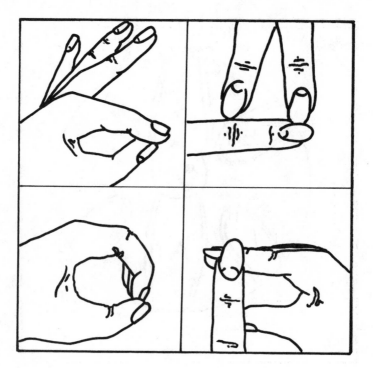

1. Use the lamp on a slide projector to provide a lighted area.

2. Using your fingers, make shadow patterns of circles, squares, and triangles on the wall. Have the children duplicate these patterns.

3. Make animal shapes with your hands—for example, rabbit, reindeer, crocodile. Have the child duplicate these shapes and talk about the animals as he makes them. The child can move his hands or fingers to make the animals talk.

VARIATION: page 60

BOTTLE FUN   Sensory-Motor

Eye-Hand Coordination / Following Directions / Size Concepts / Tactile Discrimination

1. Use an assortment of different size bottles with screw-type lids— for example, small pill bottles, spice containers, wide-mouth jars.

2. The child removes all the lids and places them on the table.

3. The child matches the lids to the jars one by one or as directed by the teacher. For example, the teacher indicates a specific bottle or lid, and the child finds the matching item.

4. Two children take turns indicating which item to match.

5. Place three to five lids of various sizes into a bag. The teacher gives oral directions. For example, "Find the biggest lid." "Find the lid that fits this bottle."

SWING A RING

Sensory-Motor

Eye-Hand Coordination / Gross Motor

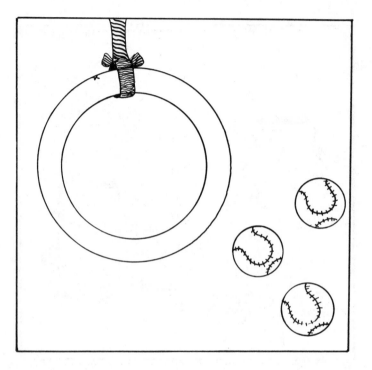

1. Attach twine to a styrofoam ring and suspend the twine from a hanger.

2. Fasten the hanger at a height, or hold and stand to one side.

3. As the ring swings back and forth, the child attempts to toss styrofoam balls through the center of the ring.

Note: A large ring of cardboard and tennis balls can be used in place of the styrofoam objects.

STRINGING STRAW   Sensory-Motor

Eye-Hand Coordination

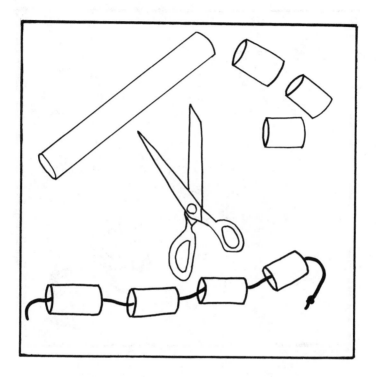

1. Cut different color plastic or paper straws into various lengths. Use large straws for young children.

2. The child uses yarn or cord to string the pieces of straw. (Dip the end of the yarn in glue to harden the tip, and knot the end of the string to hold the straws.)

3. Large macaroni can be used in the same manner. The macaroni may be painted first, so the child can string them in color patterns.

SEQUENCE NUTS AND BOLTS Sensory-Motor

Eye-Hand Coordination / Sequencing / Visual Discrimination

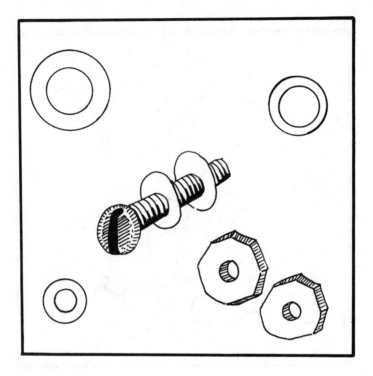

1. Use an assortment of nuts, bolts, and washers for this activity. (These can be purchased from a hardware store.)

2. Make up a variety of patterns by placing the washers and nuts on a piece of cord or a long bolt.

3. The child duplicates the pattern on another piece of cord or bolt.

Note: The items needed to duplicate each pattern can be kept with the model in a small plastic bag or placed in a compartmentalized box.

Extra nuts, bolts, washers, and screws in various sizes and lengths can be used for sorting activities.

LACING CARDS

Eye-Hand Coordination

1. Punch holes in tagboard or large index cards to form various patterns.

2. The child laces the card using yarn or string. (Dip the lacing end of the yarn or string in glue to harden it, and tie a knot in the other end to prevent it from pulling through the hole.)

3. Make additional cards for lacing patterns of letters, numbers, and shapes.

Note: Sections of pegboard can be used with lines, simple shapes, or objects painted on the pegboard.

TONG PICK-UP

Sensory-Motor

Eye-Hand Coordination / Reading

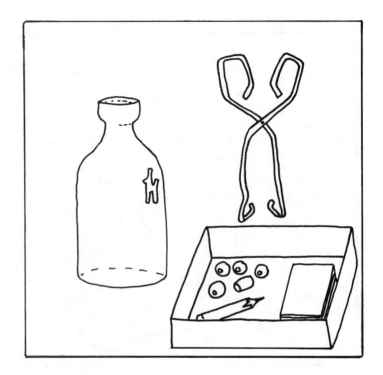

1. Place a variety of small objects on a tray—for example, beads.

2. Prepare a set of cards with the names of the objects written on them.

3. Place the cards on the tray. The child selects a card and reads the name of the object.

4. Use a small-neck plastic bottle or a box with a small hole in the top.

5. The child uses tongs, tweezers, or kitchen clamps to pick up the object and put it in the container.

6. This can be a team relay in which each child reads the name of an object, picks up the object with the tongs, and carries it to the container.

NAIL LACING

Eye-Hand Coordination

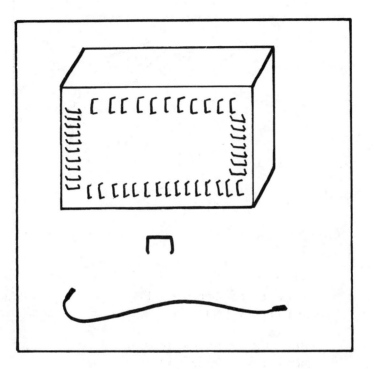

1. Pound double-pointed tacks into a board at regular intervals to make a pattern (see illustration).

2. Use yarn or long shoe laces for lacing. Tie one end of the yarn or lace to a tack.

3. The child laces through the tacks as directed—for example, "Lace under one tack and over the next."

4. Other lacing boards can be made using different patterns.

TILE PATTERNS   **Sensory-Motor**

*Eye-Hand Coordination | Part-Whole | Visual Discrimination |
Shape Recognition | Color, Form Discrimination*

1. Draw designs on large index cards, tagboard sheets, or lightweight cardboard—for example, a flower, a house, or one of the various shapes.

2. Select the tile shapes that will be used in the design and complete the design by drawing the appropriate shapes (see illustration).

3. The child selects a design and the pieces of tile that fit the shape drawn. He places them on the design. (If there is an ample supply of tiles, allow the child to glue the tiles to the design.)

4. The child can create his own design or picture and glue the tiles in place.

Note: Designs can be made on a ditto and run off on tagboard sheets.

PLACE A PIN   Sensory-Motor

Eye-Hand Coordination / Color, Form Discrimination

1. Paint or paste various colors of tape to the sides of a box to form verticle lines.

2. Using small, colored plastic clothespins, the child places the clothespins on the box matching the color of the pin to the tape.

3. The teacher can time the child in this activity.

Note: Wooden snap clothespins can be painted to match the verticle strips and used for this activity.

VARIATION: page 60

GADGET MANIPULATION Sensory-Motor

Eye-Hand Coordination / Following Directions

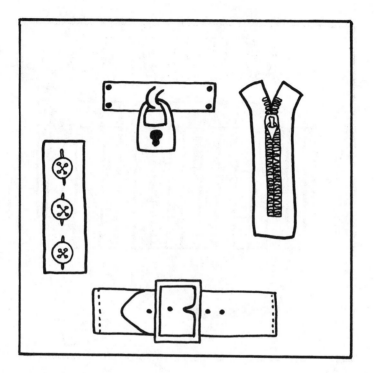

1. On a large piece of thin plywood, fasten various manipulative items—for example, zippers, button-hole strips cut from old shirts, belt buckles, hooks, padlocks, nuts and bolts.

2. Use double-pointed nails or a staple gun to attack the items.

3. The child manipulates the items according to the teacher's directions.

Note: Increase the difficulty of the task by using smaller items.

ROLL A LINE   Sensory-Motor

Eye-Hand Coordination / Color, Form Discrimination

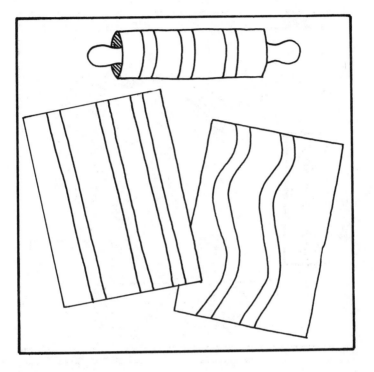

1. Draw straight, curved, and zigzag colored lines on lightweight cardboard.

2. Draw colored lines or tape colored strips on a miniature rolling pin to correspond to the colored lines on the card.

3. The child matches the colored line on the rolling pin to the line on the paper and rolls along the line following the design.

4. The child can also use a toy car or a dough cutter to trace over the design.

FINGER GOLF

Sensory-Motor

Eye-Hand Coordination / Counting / Number Sequence / Simple Computation

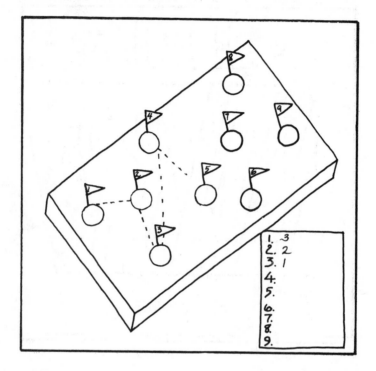

1. Drill nine shallow holes into a wooden board at various intervals.

2. Cut nine felt triangles numbered 1-9, and glue to the tops of nails. Attach nails with felt triangles to sides of holes.

3. Make a score card by marking numbers from 1-9 on an index card.

4. The child uses his index finger to flick a metal disc into the holes. (Discs can be purchased at a hardware store.)

5. The child keeps score by indicating on his score card the number of hits it takes for each hole.

Note: If disc slips off playing board, place the game in a shallow box.

FINGER CROQUET

Sensory-Motor

Eye-Hand Coordination

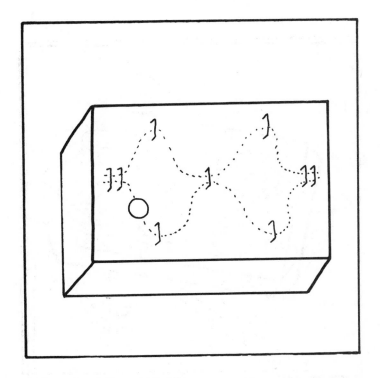

1. Pound large double-pointed tacks at various intervals on a wooden board in croquet formation.

2. The children take turns flicking metal discs through the tacks with their index finger.

3. The child who completes the course first is the winner.

4. The children can keep track of the number of tries needed for each "hoop."

Note: If discs slip off the playing board, place the game in a shallow box.

SORTING CONTAINERS   Sensory-Motor

Counting / Thinking Skills / Color, Form Discrimination / Number,
Number Group Recognition / Number Sequence

1. Nail three or more shallow tin cans onto a board and spray paint both the cans and the board.

2. Mark cans with categories—for example, number groups, numbers, and colors.

3. According to the categories indicated, the child sorts marbles, small parquet blocks, beads, alphabet macaroni, etc.

Note: Muffin tins or egg cartons can be used as sorting containers.

COLOR MATCH-UP   Sensory-Motor

Part-Whole / Concept of Half / Color Matching

1. Using those small plastic eggs that come in two parts, hide the egg halves around the room.

2. Give each child a small egg carton or basket for use in gathering the eggs.

3. The children hunt for the eggs, then match them according to color.

4. Give points for each complete egg the child assembles.

Note: This can also be an individual color matching task.

VARIATION: page 60

COLOR CONCENTRATION Sensory-Motor

Color Discrimination | Visual Memory | Color Matching

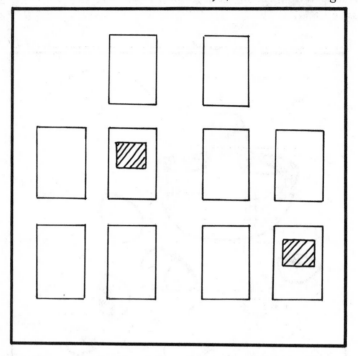

1. Paste two squares each of five different common colors of construction paper on small cards—i.e., make two red cards, two blue, etc.

2. Two children play "Concentration." The cards are placed face down in several rows.

3. One child turns over any two cards. If the two colors match, the child keeps the pair. If they do not match, the cards are turned face down again; the next child takes a turn. The child with the most cards at the end is the winner. (The child can also name the color.)

4. Make a second deck using additional colors. The two decks can also be combined after the children have played with each deck individually.

5. Card sets can be made up for shape matching.

Note: "Number Concept Cards" (p. 105) and "Deal the Deck" (p. 84) cards can also be used for "Concentration" games.

SHAPE HUNT

Shape Recognition / Figure-Ground Discrimination / 7
/ Classification

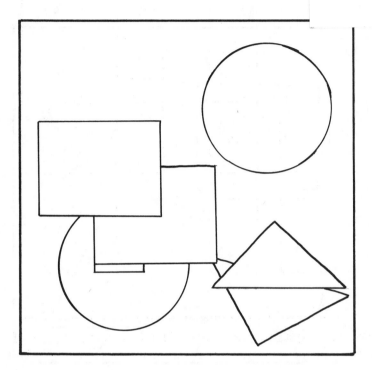

1. Cut out approximately six each of various shapes in different sizes and colors. Use circles, triangles, squares, ovals, and rectangles. (To increase level of difficulty, use diamonds, hexagons, and other shapes. To decrease level of difficulty, use just the circle, triangle, and square.)

2. Place the shapes in various places in the room.

3. The children "hunt" for the shapes.

4. After the shapes have been found, the children name other objects in the room that have the same shape. If a child has located three squares, he names three things with a square shape.

5. The same game can be played using color instead of shape.

Note: These shapes may be used for the "Sort the Stack" activity (p. 69).

43

Eye-Hand Coordination

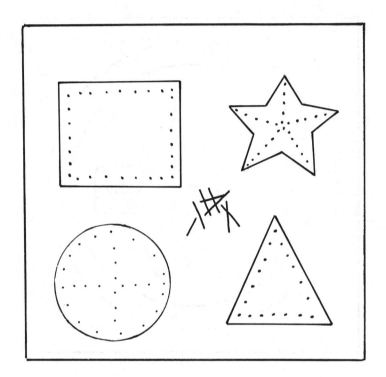

1. Use different-colored marking pens to design a dot pattern on styrofoam forms. (Styrofoam packing materials are good for this activity.)

2. The child reproduces the pattern by placing colored toothpicks in the corresponding dots.

Note: Colored golf tees may be used for this activity.

VIEW WHEEL

Sensory-Motor

Visual Memory / Letter, Word Recognition / Verbal Expression /
Number, Number Group Recognition

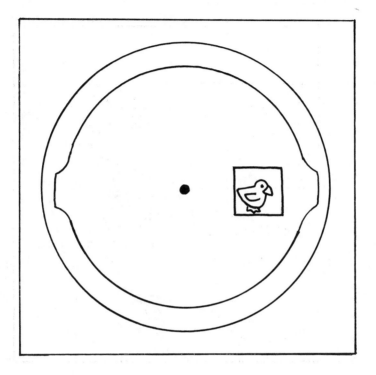

1. Cut two cardboard circles (one smaller than the other).

2. On the large circle, draw various pictures at intervals around the edge.

3. Fasten two tabs around the edge of the small circle for turning, and cut a square window near the edge of the small circle.

4. Use a small brad to fasten the two circles together.

5. Briefly expose one picture. Remove from view. Ask the child to describe the picture.

Note: View wheels can be made for number and word recognition, and phonic activities.

Part-Whole / Thinking Skills

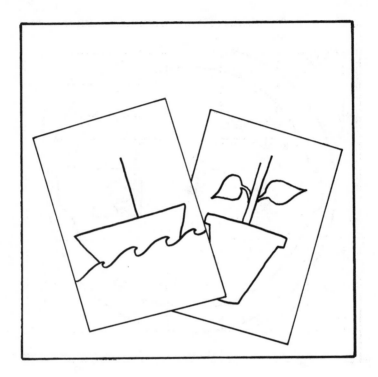

1. Prepare simple pictures with one part missing from each picture.

2a. The child identifies the missing part, then draws or cuts out the missing part from colored paper and places it in the correct position on the picture—for example, a door missing from a house, a leg missing from a table.

or

2b. Cover the pictures with contact paper or acetate sheets. The child draws in the missing part with a marking pen.

VARIATION: page 60

WHICH WAY?   Sensory-Motor

Directional Concepts / Visual Memory / Following Directions

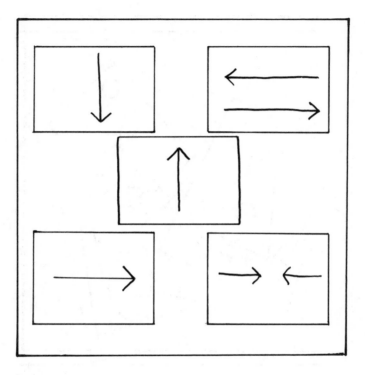

1. Prepare a series of 5″ x 8″ index cards with one or more arrows pointing in various directions.

2. As the teacher shows the cards, the child tells the direction in which the arrow is pointing.

3. The child shows the direction either by facing the same way or by pointing.

4. The child can draw the arrows shown on the cards, first while looking at them and then from memory.

Note: Make a duplicate set of cards and use as a matching activity.

DESCRIBE AND DUPLICATE   Sensory-Motor

Visual Memory / Position in Space / Verbal Expression / Tactile Discrimination

1. Draw colored lines and shapes in different positions on large index cards or tagboard sheets.

2. The child draws the design, first using the prepared card for reference and then drawing the design from memory.

3. The child describes the design when appropriate—for example, "A red triangle with a circle inside and a green line under it."

4. Cover the cards with contact paper for a tracing activity.

FELT FORMS   Sensory-Motor

Part-Whole / Eye-Hand Coordination / Verbal Expression / Body Image

1. Draw outlines of figures, objects, or animals on 5″ x 8″ index cards.

2. Cut pieces of felt to correspond to the outlined objects (see illustration).

3. The child places felt pieces on the corresponding parts shown on the cards and tells a story when the felt picture is completed.

4. To increase the difficulty, the child places felt pieces on a flannel board to form objects, using no visual model for reference.

PUZZLE PICTURES   Sensory-Motor

Part-Whole / Thinking Skills / Word Recognition

1. Mount simple pictures from magazines or old workbooks on poster board or cardboard.

2. Cut the picture cards into strips, squares, or diagonals to make puzzles.

3. The child puts the puzzle pieces together to form a picture.

Note: Add letters to spell out objects when appropriate (see illustration).

Begin with two cuts to form a puzzle and increase the number of cuts according to the child's ability.

POSITION PRACTICE   Sensory-Motor

Position in Space / Visual Discrimination

1. On two cards, draw the same simple face—but vary the position of the hairbow.

2. Instruct the child to match the cards and describe the positions of the hairbows.

3. On a separate sheet of paper, the child can draw one of the faces placing the hairbow in the same position as shown on the example.

Variation: page 61

DITTO DESIGNS   Sensory-Motor

Spatial Relationships / Color, Form Discrimination

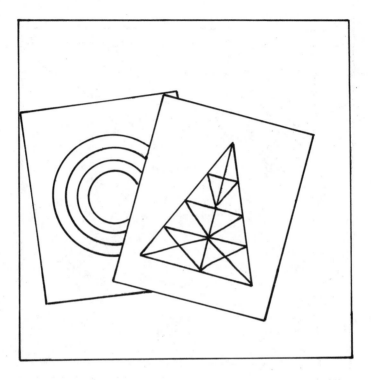

1. Prepare a variety of designs on dittos. Vary the patterns in level of complexity.

2. Have the children color these in various color patterns and mount them on cardboard.

3. After choosing one of the colored design patterns, the child duplicates the color pattern on a corresponding "blank" design sheet.

Variation: page 61

MYSTERY PICTURES   Sensory-Motor

Figure-Ground Discrimination / Number, Number Group Recognition

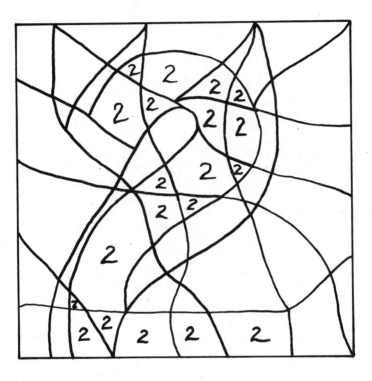

1. Prepare a ditto master as follows:

   a. Draw or stencil a large number.
   b. Draw lines dissecting the number form (see illustration).
   c. In each section of the large number, write in the same number in miniature.

2. The child colors in each numbered section of the picture.

3. The hidden form becomes apparent when the coloring is completed.

Variation: page 61

Sequencing / Following Directions / Letter Recognition

1. Mount various paragraphs on 5″ x 8″ index cards or on sheets of tagboard.

2. Laminate or cover with clear contact paper.

3. Give the child specific directions in one of the following ways:
   a. Simple symbols—for example, a *e*
   b. Printed instructions—for example, "Draw a line under each e."
   c. Verbal instructions—for example, "Draw a line through each i."

4. The child marks on the card with a washable marker, always moving from left to right.

Note: Use a variety of sizes and styles of type—for example, paragraphs from old primers, advertising copy in magazines and newspapers for larger print materials.

      Have the child find the alphabet in sequence or all the letters that make up a particular word.

GRID DESIGNS

Sensory-Motor

Part-Whole / Figure-Ground Discrimination / Following Directions

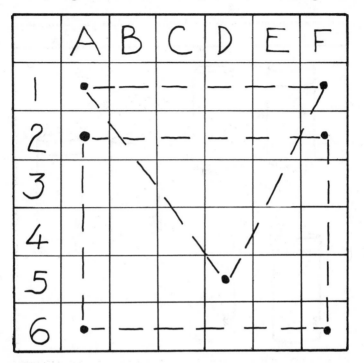

1. Prepare a ditto grid: ½″ x ½″ squares, seven spaces horizontally, seven spaces vertically.

2. Write in the letters A through F across the top and the numbers 1 through 6 down the left column (see illustration).

3. On a sheet of paper, prepare a design by placing dots in the appropriate squares. Transfer pattern to a ditto sheet.

4. Write directions for the design. For example, "Draw a straight line connecting the dot in 1A to the dot in 1F, 1F to 5D, 5D to 1A." Draw a straight line connecting the dot in 2A to the dot in 2F, 2F to 6F, 6F to 6A, 6A to 2A."

5. When the child completes the design, he colors the shapes a solid color and the remaining squares in a checkerboard pattern.

Note: The teacher may make designs for the children, or older students can develop patterns for each other and for younger children.

Auditory Discrimination

1. Fill pairs of plastic pill containers with pennies, rice, toothpicks, matches, bells, or upholstery tacks.

2. Spray paint the outside and top of each container. Leave the bottoms clear for identification.

3. The child shakes and matches the containers according to the sound heard.

Variation: page 61

ANIMAL JUMP　　　　Sensory-Moto

Gross Motor

SNAKE AND SNAIL

1. Use masking tape, chalk, or paint on oilcloth or the floor to make a snake and a snail (see illustration).
2. The children hop or jump from space to space on the patterns.
3. The children can hop on one foot, then change to the other foot, and then both feet.

OCTOPUS BROAD JUMP

1. Using the same materials suggested above, make an octopus.
2. The children jump from arm to arm.
3. The distance between each arm should increase (see illustration).

BUNNY HOP

1. Using the materials suggested above, make a bunny.
2. The children hop from space to space on the rabbit as in hopscotch.
3. Use poker chips or buttons as markers.

Variation: page 61

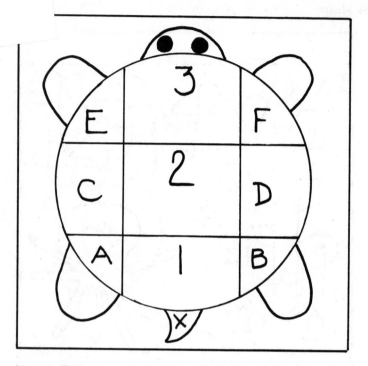

GROSS MOTOR

1. Using masking tape, chalk, or paint on oilcloths or the floor, make a turtle pattern (see illustration).
2. Standing on X the child jumps, landing on both feet in space 1.
3. Jump in stride position, landing with the left foot in space A and the right foot in space B.
4. Jump back to space 1.
5. Jump into space 2.
6. Jump in stride position, landing, with left foot in space C and right foot in space D.
7. Jump back to space 2.
8. Jump into space 3.
9. Jump in stride position, landing with left foot in space E and right foot in space F.
10. Jump back to space 3.
11. Jump out of turtle onto head.

LINE OBSTACLE COURSE   Sensory-Motor

Gross Motor / Following Directions / Reading

1. Use masking tape to make various line patterns on the floor (see illustration).

2. Number each pattern.

3. Place a book, eraser, glass of water, spoon with a marble, or pie tin with tennis ball at the start of each line pattern.

4. Write directions on index cards indicating (a) the number of the pattern to follow, (b) which object to hold, (c) whether to run, walk, or hop.

5. The child takes a card, reads the directions, then follows them.

Note: Oral instructions can be given, and objects can be omitted.

FLASHLIGHT TRACE p. 19. Two or more children can play "follow the leader" or "flashlight tag" by shining the flashlights in different parts of the room. To distinguish lights, cover the flashlights with colored cellophane.

For a listening and following directions exercise, the teacher can give verbal directions: "Shine the light to the right." "Shine it on your shoes." "Shine it on the door."

MYSTERY BOX p. 20. Play as a guessing game. One child describes the object as he feels it. The other children try to guess what it is.

TRACING CARDS p. 23. Write a simple riddle on tagboard. Fasten an envelope to the back of the tagboard with the answer in pictorial form—for example, an apple, an animal.

HAND SHADOWS p. 26. Use an old bedsheet held by two children as a screen. Place a light on one side of the sheet. The children take turns performing movements. The other children try to guess the actions.

PLACE A PIN p. 35. Number the verticle lines and the clothespins (use wooden snap clothespins). The child matches the number on the clothespin to the appropriately numbered vertical line on the box.

COLOR MATCH-UP p. 41. Put all the egg halves in a bag. The child reaches in and takes out three. If any two match, the child snaps them together and returns the third to the bag. The game continues until all the halves are matched. Encourage the children to name the colors and to identify other things in the room having the same colors.

ADD A PART p. 46. Use actual objects with missing parts—for example, a doll with a missing leg, a car with a missing wheel, a cup with a missing handle.

POSITION PRACTICE p. 51. Make additional cards showing faces with eyes looking in different directions, or a child holding a balloon in different positions, etc.

DITTO DESIGNS p. 52. Prepare color patterns on cross-section paper with ½-inch or 1-inch squares. Give the child a piece of uncolored cross-section paper and direct him to duplicate the color pattern of the example.

MYSTERY PICTURES p. 53. Use letters and shapes instead of numbers—for example, the letter A written in each section of a large A. Simple pictures can be used with the beginning letter written in each section. If the form is a ball, the letter B would appear in each section of the ball.

SHAKE AND LISTEN p. 56. Prepare several pairs of larger containers with varying amounts of sand—for example, almost empty, half full, and full. The child matches the containers according to their weight.

ANIMAL JUMP p. 57. Place small objects in the spaces, to be picked up in one space and put down in the next. Use direction cards at the sides of the spaces indicating that the child should change feet or jump backwards.

PART THREE
LANGUAGE

LANGUAGE

The language section emphasizes auditory skills, verbal expression, and reading and phonics activities. In conjunction with the materials presented in this section, the teacher must provide a wide variety of concrete experiences. These might include the use of the tape recorder, field trips, and creative dramatics.

An attempt has been made to present the items according to the level of complexity and the major skills area involved. The general order of the items is as follows:

Letter and word identification

Classification

Beginning sounds

Rhyming words

Following directions

Listening skills

Thinking skills

Verbal expression

Sentence construction

Many of the variations in this section contain arithmetic ideas.

PARK AND STOP Language

Word Recognition / Color, Form Discrimination / Listening / Follow-
ing Directions

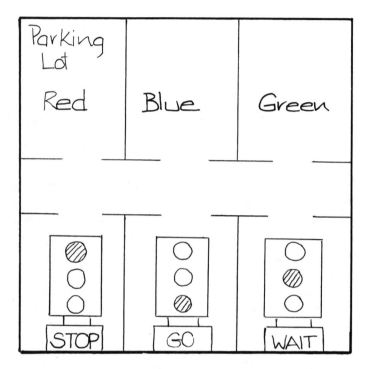

1. Using colored paper, cut out different colored squares. Paste on tagboard to make a parking lot.

2. Draw stoplights at the bottom of the paper (see illustration).

3. Use miniature cars the same color as the parking lots.

4. The child moves a car on the paper according to the teacher's directions—for example, "Drive the blue car to the blue parking lot." "Drive the red car to the yellow light."

QUICK CALL Language

Letter, Word Recognition / Letter, Word Matching

1. Prepare a deck of cards with several sets of identical letters or words.

2. Shuffle cards and deal to two children.

3. The children simultaneously turn over one card at a time.

4. When two identical cards turn up, the child who first names the letter or word takes both turned-up stacks of cards.

5. The game is won when one child gets all the cards.

VARIATION: page 99

ALPHABET SCRATCH   Language

Letter, Word Recognition

1. Write the letters of the alphabet on a strip of 2" x 8" tagboard. Cover with contact paper.

2. Prepare a set of word cards, using *all* the letters of the alphabet—for example, puzzle, exit, quiet.

3. Place the word cards on the center of the table.

4. The game is played by two or four children, each using his own alphabet strip.

5. The first child selects a card—for example, BOX. He may cross out two of the three letters on his alphabet strip. This applies to all subsequent words as well; the child crosses out *all but one* of the letters in each word, regardless of length.

6. The game continues in this manner until one child has crossed out all his letters.

Note: Cards can be wiped off and reused.

68

SORT THE STACK   Language

Classification / Color, Form Discrimination / Thinking Skills

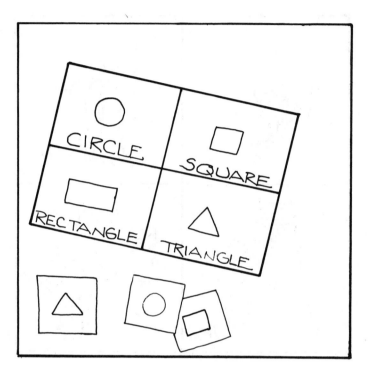

1. Divide a large card into four sections.

2. Indicate a category in each section—for example, zoo animals, farm animals, shapes, types of food.

3. Prepare picture cards relating to these categories.

4. The child matches the picture cards to the corresponding categories.

VARIATION: page 99

SEASONAL SORT   Language

Classification / Thinking Skills / Verbal Expression

1. Prepare a large playing card with four sections.

2. Draw or paste a picture associated with each of the four seasons in each section.

3. Prepare a smaller set of cards with seasonal themes. These seasonal pictures correspond to those on the playing card—for example, swimming pool, snow scene, haystack.

4. The child selects a small card, names the season represented, and places the card on the appropriate section of the playing card.

5. The child can give a sentence about the season or tell a story.

Note: Before playing the game, be sure the children understand the symbols for each season.

ASSOCIATION PICTURES   Language

Verbal Expression / Word Association

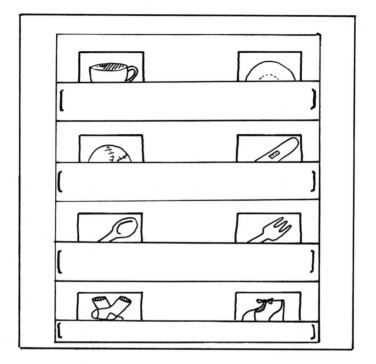

1. Mount individual pictures of objects commonly associated with each other on small cards—for example, cup-saucer, ball-bat, shoe-sock. (Rather than search for specific pictures, use association pages from reading readiness workbooks.)

2. Use a work chart with slots in it or make a card holder with strips of tagboard stapled to a larger tagboard piece.

3. Place a picture in each slot down the left hand side of the chart.

4. Give the child a group of pictures to be matched.

5. The child places the matching pictures in the same slot and tells how the two are associated.

Note: These cards can also be used in "Concentration" or "Deal the Deck" (p. 84) games.

SEQUENCE CARDS   Language

Part-Whole / Sequencing / Verbal Expression

1. Mount on small cards individual pictures that form a sequence when placed in order.
2. Some sets can be two-part sequences, others three or four parts, up to sequences of nine or ten parts.
3. The child arranges the cards in order or the teacher has the set partially arranged and asks, "Which card would fit here?"
4. The child tells a story or tells his reasoning for each sequence.

Note: Picture sets can be found in reading readiness workbooks, science workbooks, before-after advertisements, and comic strips.

VARIATION: page 99

ABSURD PICTURES   Language

Verbal Expression / Thinking Skills / Observing Detail

1a. Collect an assortment of pictures showing some absurdity or error. (Many advertisements have appropriate pictures—for example, a woman drinking from an oversize cup of coffee, a man floating down into a rental car. Human interest stories in newspapers and picture magazines are often another source—for example, an incorrect sign, a freak photograph.

or

1b. Make simple line drawings showing absurdities—for example, a boy with flowers growing out of his head, a clock face with the numbers going counterclockwise.

2. Use the pictures as a basis for discussion. The children locate the error, tell why it is incorrect, and what it should be.

Visual Discrimination / Figure-Ground Discrimination

1. Mount individual pictures on 9″ x 12″ tagboard sheets. Use pictures showing a variety of objects.

2. Write simple directions at the bottom of each sheet—for example, "Find two birds." "Find something blue." "Find something that begins with m." "Find something round." "Find something that can run." Mark each item a different color.

3. Laminate or cover the card with contact paper.

4. The child must read the direction and mark the item with the color indicated. (Use a washable marker or wax crayon so it can be rubbed off and the card reused.)

Note: Give verbal directions to children who cannot read.

       Add pictures to this collection gradually as you find appropriate ones rather than trying to assemble an entire group at once.

Initial Sounds

1. Prepare 40 domino-like cards on 1″ x 2″ pieces of tagboard. For example, choose ten different letters of the alphabet and write a letter on one half of each card. On the other half of the card, place a picture that begins with any of the ten letters. (The letter and picture on the same card do not match.)

2. If there are four B letter cards, there should be four B picture cards.

3. The child plays "Dominoes" matching the letters and pictures according to the initial sounds.

VARIATION: page 99

SPACE FILL-IN

Language

Part-Whole / Letter Recognition

1. Cut body parts out of felt to form a picture of an astronaut.

2. On a sheet of paper or the chalkboard, make a line for each letter of a word related to the picture—for example, — — — — (MOON).

3. The child guesses a letter and writes the letter anywhere on the paper or chalk board.

   a. If the letter selected is in the word, the teacher places the letter on the dashed line.

   b. If the letter is not in the word, the child begins to assemble the astronaut figure using felt cutouts.

   c. For every letter guessed that is not in the word, another part of the figure is added.

   d. The game is over when the astronaut figure is completed or the word has been guessed.

Note: Several children can play the game with one of the children as leader.

ADD THE LETTER

Language

Initial Sounds / Word Recognition

1. Make a set of word cards. Omit the first letter of each word, and draw a picture that illustrates the word (see illustration).

2. Prepare a set of 1″ x 1″ alphabet cards.

3. The child selects the correct letter from the alphabet cards to fill in the missing letter on the word card.

Note: Sets of cards can be made omitting medial and final letters.

The word cards can be covered with clear contact paper, and the child can fill in the missing letter with a marking pen.

JUMBLED WORDS

Language

Sequencing / Word Recognition

1. Prepare a set of cards, each containing a picture and jumbled letters to the corresponding word. Cover the cards with clear contact paper.

2. Using the picture clue to determine the correct word, the child sounds out the letter order.

3. The child may write the correct word directly on the card with a washable marker or use letter cards to form the word.

Note: To increase the difficulty, use jumbled letters without a stimulus picture.

Shape, Letter, Word Recognition / Visual Memory

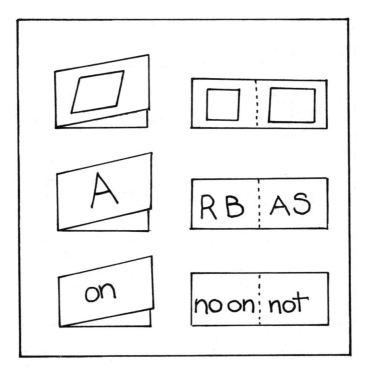

1. Fold strips of 2″ x 8″ tagboard in half.

2. On the front, draw a shape, letter, or word.

3. On the inside, put a duplicate of the front marking along with one or more other figures.

4. The child observes the item on the front briefly, then turns to the inside to locate the duplicate.

HANG-UP RELAY Language

Letter, Word Recognition / Sequencing

1. Write simple words on 3″ x 5″ index cards.
2. Make two sets of 2″ x 3″ alphabet cards and punch holes in the top.
3. Cut two 2″ x 15″ boards out of pressed board. Fasten cup hooks every 2 inches near the top of the boards.
4. Divide the class into two teams. The teams stand a distance from the chalk board with their alphabet cards in view.
5. The teacher holds up a stimulus card—for example, HOUSE.
6. One child from each team selects the beginning letter from the alphabet cards and places it on the first hook on the left of his team board.
7. The relay continues with other team members adding letters to complete the word.

Note: Make extra letters for those used often.

POSTAL SORT   Language

Letter Recognition / Letter Matching / Initial Sounds / Classification

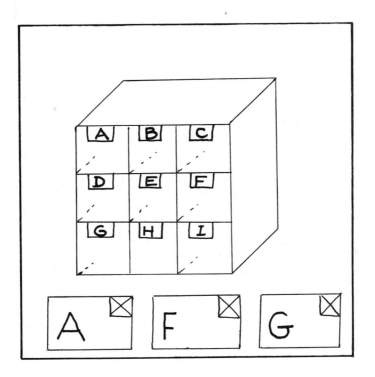

1. Turn a sectional packing box on its side, and tape small letter tabs to each section.

2. Prepare a set of cards to match the tabs used on the box.

3. The child sorts the cards according to the tabs on the sectional packing box.

Note: The cards can be made to look like postal cards by placing used stamps or seals at the top right of the card.

VARIATION: page 99

CHECK A WORD

Language

Letter, Word Recognition / Verbal Expression

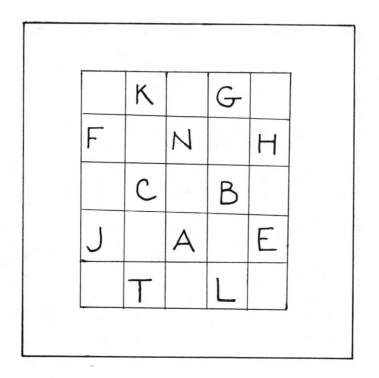

1. Make a checkerboard, or use a commercial board.

2. Write letters or words in the squares (see illustration).

3. Using poker chips, buttons, or beans for markers, the child plays "Checkers"—he must be able to say the letter or word in the square to which he wants to move.

VARIATION: page 100

COMPOUND LOTTO

Language

Compound Word Recognition

1. Prepare several playing cards with six to nine spaces.

2. On the left side of each space, write the first part of a common compound word. (Use different words on each playing card.)

3. Prepare small cards with the second part of each compound word. Place the small cards face down on a flat surface.

4. The children take turns turning over cards.

5. If the small word card matches a compound word on the playing card, the child plays the card in that space.

6. If the word card does not match, he places it face down.

Note: Prepare other card sets with rhyming words and opposites.

DEAL THE DECK

Language

*Letter, Word Recognition / Initial, Medial, Final Sounds / Rhyming
/ Letter, Word Matching*

1. Prepare card decks of similar combinations—for example, capital
   and lower case letters, opposites, rhyming words, contractions.

2. Shuffle and deal an equal number of cards to each child.

3a. Each child draws a card in turn from the other children's hands
    and forms pairs.

or

3b. The child may ask for certain cards instead of drawing—for ex-
    ample, "Do you have the contraction for *is not* (*isn't*) ?"

4. The game continues until all cards have been paired.

VARIATION: page 100

REACH YOUR GOAL Language

Letter, Word Recognition / Initial Sounds / Verbal Expression

1. Draw game boards with a magic marker on tagboard or poster board. Themes will provide added interest for the child.

2. Make small cards containing letters, words, pictures, or beginning sounds.

3. The child draws a card from the stack. When he correctly identifies it, he moves his marker one space toward the finish line.

Note: If the game board is designed to be a race track, have the child move a small car toward the finish line.

VARIATION: page 100

WORD BLENDER

Language

Blends / Word Recognition

1. Write word blends on 40 or 50 cards (one word per card).
2. Cut the word card in two, separating the blend from the rest of the word.
3. Shuffle the blend cards and place them face down on the table. Shuffle the word cards and place them face down beside the blend cards.
4. Two or four children can play this game.
5. The first child picks one card from each stack. If he thinks the blend fits the letters on the word card, he says the word and places the cards together. If he is correct, he keeps the cards.
6. If the blend and letters do not form a word, he places each card on the bottom of its stack.
7. The child with the most cards wins the game.

Spelling / Visual Discrimination

1. The child selects and cuts out a picture from an old magazine.

2. The child lists the objects in the picture on a sheet of paper.

3. The child should use a dictionary for correct spelling of the objects.

4. The child may write a synonym or antonym for each object on his list.

Note: Suggest a number of words consistent with the child's ability. These words can be used for the child's individualized spelling list for the week.

FUNNY SENTENCE

Parts of Speech

My teacher told me to go
_____ and finish my school _____.
NOUN   NOUN
I _____ all the way _____ . I _____
   VERB   NOUN   VERB
the door and _____ a _____
                       VERB   ADJECTIVE
bowl of cookies on the _____ .
                                       NOUN
I _____ tiptoed over to the
   ADVERB
_____ jar. I was just
ADJECTIVE
getting ready to _____ a
                              VERB
cookie when I heard _____ .
                                    NOUN

1. Write a short story using a theme of interest to children. Omit the nouns, verbs, adjectives, and adverbs.

2. Draw a line in the space where the omitted words should appear, and write the type of word to be inserted below the line (see illustration).

3. Prepare a ditto listing the rules that apply to nouns, verbs, adjectives, or adverbs—for example, "Noun—names a person, place, or thing."

4. The teacher reads the story. When a blank appears, she calls on a child to fill in the blank with the appropriate noun, verb, adjective, or adverb.

5. Continue this procedure until the story is completed, then select a child to read the story to the class.

Note: Have the children write their own stories. When reading the story to the class, the teacher eliminates certain words, indicates the parts of speech, and calls on class members to fill in the blanks.

FELT FUN

Listening / Reading / Counting / Auditory Discrimination / Shape Recognition / Following Directions

1. Use different colored felt pieces to make a variety of small objects or shapes.

2. Prepare cards with lists of simple directions—for example, "two green trees," "one red apple," "three white rabbits."

3. The child places objects on the flannel board after either listening to the teacher's directions or reading from the card.

WHAT TO WEAR WHEN   Language

Thinking Skills / Directional Concepts / Auditory Discrimination / Listening / Following Directions

1. Make boy and girl figures from felt.

2. Prepare simple articles of clothing covering seasonal and weather changes, different times of the day, and different occasions.

3. Use marking pens to make details—for example, buttons, shoe laces, and collars.

4. Make articles such as mittens and shoes to correspond to the right and left sides.

5. The children dress the dolls as they wish or as the teacher directs —for example, "Dress the girl doll for a rainy day." "Put a red dress, white socks, and black shoes on the girl doll."

VARIATION: page 100

POP-UP   Language

Sequencing / Word Recognition

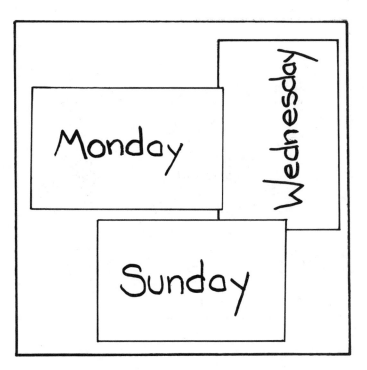

1. Prepare a set of large cards containing the days of the week (one day per card).

2. Each child has one or more cards.

3. The teacher asks, "What comes before Tuesday?"

4. The child holding the correct card "pops up" and says the name.

5. The children can move with their cards to show the sequence of the days of the week.

VARIATION: page 100

MOTIVATIONAL ASSIGNMENTS Language

Following Directions

1. Draw various shapes on a tagboard sheet.
2. Cut out shapes and fold to make flaps. Designs, shapes, and seasonal themes can be drawn on the flaps.
3. Staple the cut-out tagboard to another piece the same size.
4. Number the flaps.
5. Open the flaps and write the task to be completed by the child— for example, flap 1, arithmetic; flap 2, language; flap 3, game.
6. The child receives a worksheet for each task written under the flaps.
7. The child opens the first flap and completes the worksheet designated in the opening.

Note: Prepare several motivational sheets with the order of the tasks changed. These sheets can be alternated with the children. These motivational sheets are good for Learning Centers.

DIRECTION DRIVE   Language

Following Directions / Position in Space / Directional Concepts / Auditory Discrimination

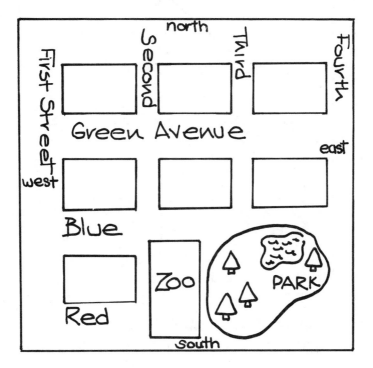

1. On a large piece of tagboard, prepare a diagram similar to the illustration and cover it with clear contact paper.

2. Give directions orally or write on index cards and give to the child to read—for example, "Drive two blocks on Blue Street, turn right, then drive three blocks on Second Avenue."

3. Using a toy car, the child follows the directions he has heard or read.

Verbal Expression / Thinking Skills / Classification

1. Prepare a set of word cards and a set of picture cards. (Pictures can be directly related to units being studied in class.)

2. Choose two teams. Give each team a picture and its corresponding word.

3. Each team member must tell something different about the picture.

4. The teams receive points according to how many sentences they are able to give about the picture.

5. The game is over when several pictures have been used.

Note: Objects may be used instead of pictures.

THREE LITTLE WORDS   Language

Verbal Expression / Thinking Skills / Word Recognition

1. Prepare a set of small cards, each containing three related words.

2. The child takes a card and makes up a sentence or a short story including all the words that appear on the card.

Note: To increase the difficulty, use words less closely related or increase the number of words.

BUILD YOUR OWN   Language

Sentence Construction / Parts of Speech / Sequencing

1. Prepare small cards with nouns, verbs, and adjectives.
2. Punch holes in the cards. Group all nouns together on one ring, verbs on another, and adjectives on a third.
3. Attach card sets to a folded cardboard stand.
4. The child flips each card set separately to form appropriate sentences.

Note: Sentence complexity may be increased by using more card sets—for example, articles, prepositions.

        The children can make up nonsense sentences and discuss why they are incorrect.

MOVE IN ORDER Language

Sentence Construction / Parts of Speech / Sequencing

1. Write various simple sentences on the outside of business size envelopes (one sentence per envelope).

2. Place small cards inside each envelope, each card containing one word of the sentence.

3. Divide the class into groups, and give each group an envelope. (The number of children in the group must correspond to the number of words in their envelope.)

4. Each child takes a word from the envelope. Holding their words, the children arrange themselves in sentence sequence. (If necessary, the children may use the sentence written on the envelope as a clue.)

QUIZ CARDS   Language

Verbal Expression / Thinking Skills / Listening / Auditory Discrimination

1. Prepare general or subject area questions on 3″ x 5″ index cards—for example, science, transportation, famous people, places.

2. Divide the children into two teams.

3. The team members alternate taking cards from the stack.

4. Each child reads a question and responds in sentence form.

5. For each correct answer, the team receives a point.

QUICK CALL p. 67. Use with number concept cards, alphabet cards, shapes, designs, and colors.

SORT THE STACK p. 69. Prepare a set of sorting cards with letters and words. If two or more children play, they can use colored discs or markers to indicate the category correctly guessed. The markers are counted at the end of the game.

SEQUENCE CARDS p. 72. On a series of cards, draw a completion sequence—for example, a stick figure, adding one body part each card; a face, gradually adding more features; a shape, adding one more line per card.

PHONETIC DOMINOES p. 75. The game is simplified by preparing a set of domino-type cards with letters only, shapes, or colors. The child matches the letters.

POSTAL SORT p. 81. Prepare cards with simple addresses—for example, "8 Brown Street." Place corresponding tabs on the box. Prepare other sets of cards with pictures. The child sorts the pictures according to the beginning sound.

CHECK A WORD p. 72. Prepare a checkerboard with pictures in the squares. Have the child name the beginning sound or say a sentence about the picture before he can move his marker to that square.

DEAL THE DECK p. 84. Prepare sets of cards with shapes, number groups, and number combinations—for example, "2 + 2" and "4."

REACH YOUR GOAL p. 85. Use with number concept cards, alphabet cards, arithmetic flash cards, shape and design identification cards. With arithmetic flash cards the child would move the number of spaces indicated on the card—for example, 3 + 3, the child moves six spaces.
Halloween Trick or Treat. Prepare game card with Halloween motif. Winner receives a treat. Other players must do a trick.

WHAT TO WEAR WHEN? p. 90. Make doll clothes for a large doll. Use various regular size buttons, snaps, and zippers. The children learn to manipulate these things by dressing the doll. Costumes can be made for the children and used in the same way.

POP-UP p. 91. Prepare a card set with numbers. The teacher asks, "What comes before 7?" Prepare a set of alphabet cards and use as above. The child responds by "popping up."

PART FOUR
NUMBER CONCEPTS

NUMBER CONCEPTS

The arithmetic section emphasizes understanding of basic arithmetic and measurement concepts and computational skills.

To effectively utilize these materials, the teacher must provide opportunities for manipulation of objects, physical movement, and other concrete experiences.

As with the other sections, items are presented according to the level of complexity and the major concept involved. The general order of the items is as follows:

Numeral and number group identification

Formation of numerals

Recognition and formation of shapes

One-to-one correspondence

Counting and number sequence

Simple computation

Time, direction, and quantity concepts

Many of the variations in this section contain language ideas.

NUMBER CONCEPT CARDS Number Concepts

Classification / Number, Number Group Recognition / Number Sequence / Counting

1. Prepare sets of number groups, number words, and numerals from 1 to 10 on small cards. For the number group cards, use objects, shapes, or seals to designate number.

2. The child sorts the cards according to the teacher's directions—for example, "Find all the 2s." "Put the cards in order from 1 to 10."

Note: The cards can be used as flash cards for quick recall or in various number games.

VARIATION: page 130

STEP AND CLAP   Number Concepts

Gross Motor / Counting / Number, Number Group Recognition / Number Sequence

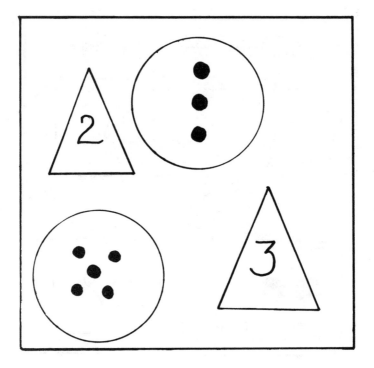

1. Cut large shapes from cardboard. Put numerals on some shapes and dot configurations on the rest (see illustration).

2. Tape the cards to the floor in sequence.

3. The child steps from card to card clapping his hands or tapping his foot the number of times indicated on the card.

VARIATION: page 130

CALENDAR MATH   Number Concepts

Counting / Sequencing / Spelling

1. Use a large calendar and make a die.

2. The first child rolls the die and moves a marker the indicated number of spaces, beginning with day one.

3. The child tells the day of the week he has landed on and spells that day.

4. If a child cannot spell the day of the week, he moves back one space.

5. The first child to reach the end of the month wins the game.

Simple Computation / Number, Number Group Recognition

1. Cut out sets of fish from colored paper. Put a paper clip on each fish.

2. Write a simple addition problem on each fish.

3. Use dowels, string, and miniature magnets to make the fishing poles.

4. Place the fish on the floor. Using a fishing pole, the child catches a fish by touching the magnet to the paper clip on the fish.

5. If the child gives the correct answer, he keeps the fish. If not, he returns the fish to the "pond."

VARIATION: page 130

Simple Computation

1. Write process signs on 1½" x 1½" cards. Prepare ten cards with the minus sign (−) and ten cards with plus (+). If older children play, include the multiplication sign (×).
2. Place a deck of playing cards in the center of the table. Remove all face cards and jokers. The ace is counted as one.
3. Place the stack of process cards beside the playing deck.
4. Two or four children can play this game.
5. The first player takes two playing cards and one process card. If the child picks a 7 and 9 and a minus (−) process card, he subtracts (9−7). If the answer is correct, he keeps the cards. If the answer is incorrect, he places the cards at the bottom of their decks.
6. Older children can take from three to five cards and work the problems.
7. The game continues in this manner until all the playing cards have been used. The child with the most cards wins.

Note: A circle spinner can be made with a piece of tagboard and a brad fastened in the center. The process signs can be written on the tagboard circle.

BUTTON DICE

Number Concepts

Simple Computation / Number, Number Group Recognition

1. Prepare a set of dice with dot configurations on them for younger children. For older children, prepare a set with the numbers on them. (Wooden squares are available in catalogs to make your own dice.)

2. Each child receives 20-30 buttons or beans.

3. The first child rolls the dice and tells which is the smaller number. For example, if he rolls a 5 and 4, he would say "Four" and then place four buttons in the pot.

4. Any child who rolls doubles may take the total of the dice from the pot.

5. When the game is over, the children count their buttons and the child with the most buttons wins the game.

VARIATION: *page 130*

MAKE A RUN   Number Concepts

Simple Computation / Number, Number Group Recognition

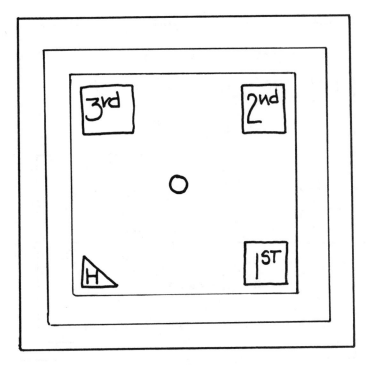

1. Prepare individual playing cards resembling baseball diamonds on 9″ x 9″ squares of tagboard.

2. The child responds to arithmetic flash cards (number recognition or arithmetic problems).

3. As correct answers are given, the child moves from base to base.

4. A point is given each time the child "makes a run."

5. The children keep track of their scores.

VARIATION: page 130

Counting / Following Directions / Number, Number Group Recognition / Number Sequence

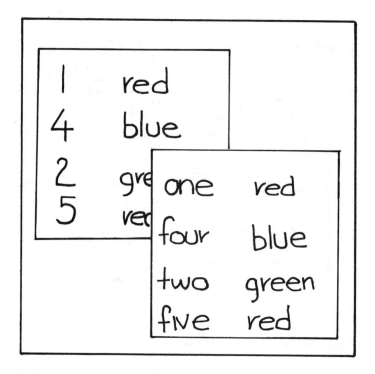

1. Prepare a series of cards with directions for bead stringing.

2. The number on the card indicates the number of beads to be strung for that color.

3. At the beginning level, use actual color cues.

4. To increase the difficulty of the task, use only color and number words in the directions.

Number, Number Group Recognition

1. Prepare a ditto master containing 3″ x 3″ grids.

2. Run off multiple copies and fasten to tagboard. (A grid may cover a 9″ x 12″ sheet or two grids may be drawn on a single master and the tagboard sheets cut apart.)

3. Mark different numerals, set configurations, or number words in the grid squares.

4. The teacher calls out numbers or shows numerals and sets to the children. The children cover only one example with markers (beans or buttons) each time.

5. The game continues until one child has covered a vertical, horizontal, or diagonal row.

Note: Prepare ditto masters with 4″ x 4″ and 5″ x 5″ grids. Mark with numerals only. Use with sets of math flash cards for addition, subtraction, multiplication, or division facts.

VARIATION: page 131

Number, Number Group Recognition / Number Matching

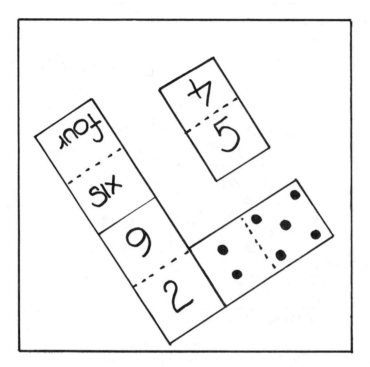

1. Prepare 40 domino-like cards approximately 1½″ by 3″.

2. Write a numeral, set configuration, or number word on each card half. Each item for 0 - 6 concepts will be used approximately four times.

3. The child plays "Dominoes" placing the cards end to end to form matches.

4. Prepare a second set of 40 cards using numerals and number words from 1 - 10. The child matches numerals and number words.

5. Other domino sets can be prepared with number facts and numerals—for example, 1 - 6, approximately 36 cards (4 examples of each) ; 7 - 10, 40 cards (3 examples of each) .

COLOR BY NUMBER   Number Concepts

Simple Computation / Number, Number Group Recognition

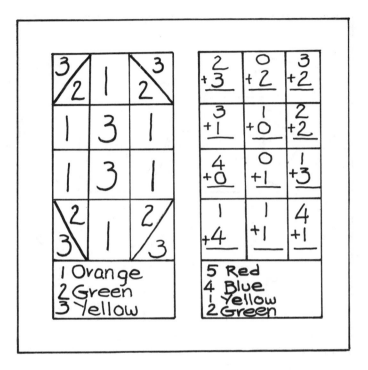

1. Make dittos of grids.

2. Place numbers in the grid spaces in a pattern. Write in a color key under the grid.

3. The child colors each space according to the color key—for example, if the number is 1, color the space orange.

4. Simple arithmetic problems can be written on the ditto. The spaces are colored in according to the answer—for example, with 2 + 3 the answer is 5, and the space is colored red.

5. Subtraction instead of addition problems can be written.

TURN-UP   Number Concepts

Simple Computation / Number Recognition

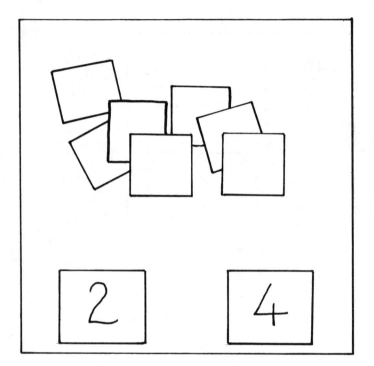

1. Prepare approximately 40 small cards with numbers from 1 and 10 written on each.

2. Turn the cards face down on a flat surface.

3. The child turns up two cards.

4. If he can add the two numbers together, he keeps the cards.

5. The game continues until all the cards have been used.

Note: This game can be used with subtraction. It can be used for column addition if the child turns over three or more cards.

COUNT, COLOR, AND ADD Number Concepts

Simple Computation / Counting / Number Sequence

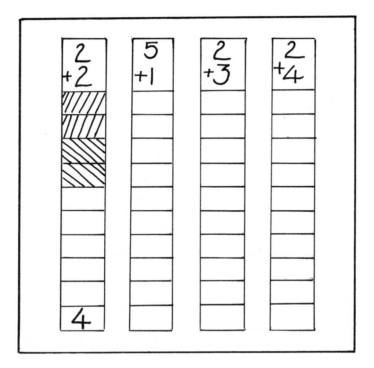

1. Make dittos of columns of boxes (see illustration).

2. Write problems in the larger boxes at the top of the page.

3. The child colors the boxes—for example, in the problem 2 + 2, the child colors two boxes one color and two boxes a different color.

4. The child counts the total number of the boxes colored and writes the answer in the larger box at the bottom of the column.

DOT SEQUENCE   Number Concepts

*Counting / Number, Number Group Recognition / Number Sequence
Eye-Hand Coordination*

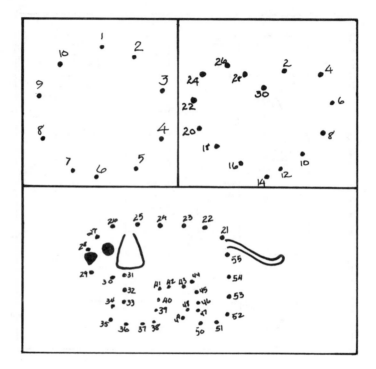

1. Make dittos of a dot and number series of shapes or simple figures.

2. The degree of difficulty is determined by the numbers used—for example, 1-10, 1-40, numbers above 100.

3. Make additional dittos for counting by 2s, 5s, and 10s.

4. Use ABCs in a sequence instead of numbers.

Simple Computation

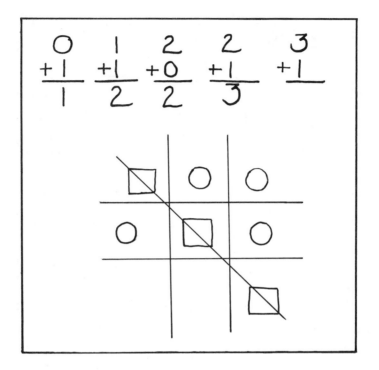

1. Two children play a regular "tic-tac-toe" game. As each child wins or loses, he adds 1 or 0 to his score.

2. The children keep a running account of their scores.

3. This game can be adapted for counting by 2s, 5s, or 10s.

4. The same scoring method can be used with ring toss or various target games.

Note: Cut colored paper circles and squares to designate playing markers for each child.

MATH DICE   Number Concepts

Simple Computation / Number Recognition / Number Formation

1. Two small wooden blocks are marked with numerals and/or number groupings.

2. Place a different number on each face of the cubes.

3. Another block is marked with plus and minus signs.

4. The child rolls the cubes. He writes out his own arithmetic problems according to the numbers and process sign that are face up on the blocks.

VARIATION: page 131

Simple Computation / Gross Motor

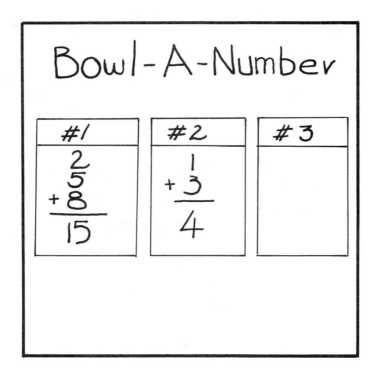

1. Prepare a bowling game using plastic bottles weighted with sand. Write or tape a number (1 - 10) on each bottle. (Commercial bowling sets can be purchased.)

2. The child bowls a game. He keeps score by adding the numbers on the fallen pins. For example, if with his first ball the child knocks down the 2, 5, and 8 pins, his score would be 15.

DAY BY DAY BINGO   Number Concepts

Number Recognition / Time Concepts

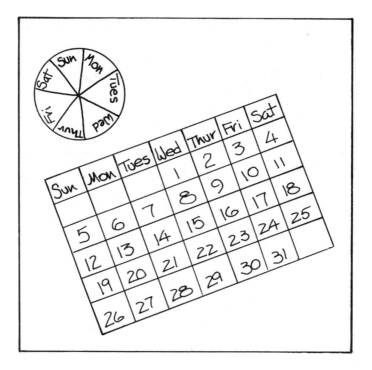

1. Use pages from an old calendar as playing cards.
2. Cut off the name of the month and mount the rest of the page on lightweight cardboard.
3. Make number chips from 1 to 31 (approximately three of each number.)
4. Make a spinner device with the days of the week on the outside of the circle.
5. The teacher picks a number chip, spins to determine the day of the week, and calls out the combination—for example, Friday, the 4th.
6. Each child covers the corresponding space on his cards.
7. The first child to complete a row either vertically or horizontally wins the game.

CALENDAR FUN   Number Concepts

*Counting / Number, Number Group Recognition / Number Sequence
/ Time Concepts*

1. Make a calendar with holiday and seasonal themes—for example,
   colored Easter eggs with numbers; a tree with numbered leaves.

2. The child places the correct number on the calendar each day.

3. Use the calendar for counting and number recognition.

MOTIVATIONAL FILL-INS Number Concepts

Simple Computation

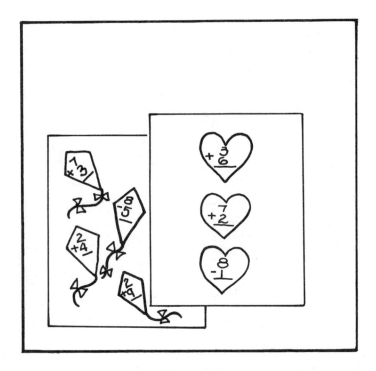

1. Prepare ditto sheets using seasonal or holiday themes.

2. The areas in the patterns are left blank.

3. The teacher fills in these areas with arithmetic problems.

4. Each child works the problems on his sheet.

YARDSTICK RACE   Number Concepts

Measurement

1. Cut a number of colored paper strips into various lengths of complete inches.
2. Place the strips between two pieces of cardboard or a large book so that approximately one inch of each strip is showing.
3. Give each child a yardstick. (These can often be obtained from various businesses in town.)
4. The child pulls out a strip of paper, places it over his yardstick to measure the length and places a poker chip or makes a mark at that point. (If the yardsticks are covered with a clear varnish, the marks can be rubbed away.) The child should count and name the number of inches moved each time.
5. The child who reaches the end of the yardstick first is the winner.
6. Increase the difficulty by having the child measure the paper strip with a ruler and then move on the yardstick without placing the paper strip on it.
7. As the children become more familiar with measuring, use paper strips that are not "even" inches—for example, $4\frac{1}{2}''$ or $3\frac{3}{4}''$.
8. A set of cards could be made with the measurements written out. For added interest, include cards such as "Go back 3 inches."

DIRECTIONAL BINGO   Number Concepts

Directional Concepts / Number Recognition

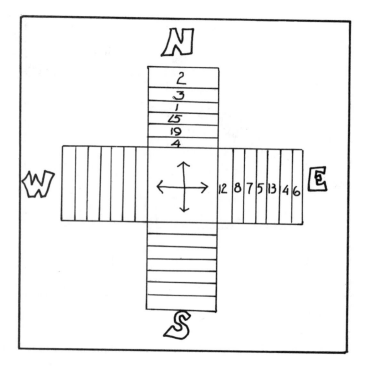

1. Prepare ditto sheets with a compass pattern (see illustration).

2. In the spaces on the playing sheet, write numbers from 1 to 20—
   numbers are not in sequence.

3. Make a set of calling chips to correspond—for example, 2N, 8E,
   9S.

4. Like "Bingo," the game is played by covering the numbers as
   called with colored discs.

5. The first child to complete a row either vertically (N-S) or horizontally (E-W) wins the game.

6. The degree of difficulty is increased by using eight directions—
   adding SE, SW, NE, NW.

NUMBER HANG-UP   Number Concepts

Place Value

1. Make four sets of numbers from 0 - 9.

2. Punch a hole in the top of 3″ x 5″ index cards.

3. Screw cup hooks into 3″ x 15″ pressed board.

4. Place the words "Thousands," "Hundreds," "Tens," and "Ones" from left to right above the hooks.

5. The card sets are placed on a table in separate stacks (1s, 2s . . . 8s, 9s) .

6. The teacher calls a number such as 8,513.

7. The child takes the correct numbers needed from the stacks and places each number on the correct hook corresponding to the place value.

PLACE VALUE DICE   Number Concepts

Place Value

1. Write numbers on six or seven dice.
2. Make dittos of a grid 1″ x 1″. Write the place value of each column at the top.
3. The child receives a grid and the dice.
4. He rolls the dice and places them above any of the spaces.
5. He then writes the number from the dice in the space provided (see illustration).
6. He reads the correct number by referring to the place value written at the top of the page.
7. He repeats the above procedure, reads the number, and then adds the two columns together and reads the new number.
8. This process is repeated until the child has completed several problems.

Measurement / Matching

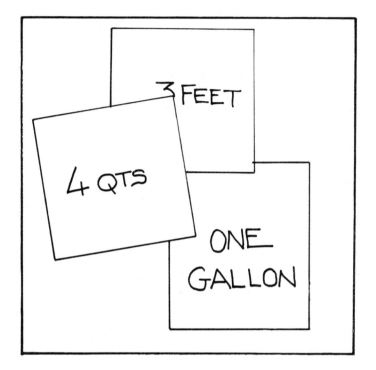

1. Prepare a deck of cards, four each of every card with one measurement per card—for example, 4 qts., 1 gal.; 2 lbs., 32 oz.; 5,280 ft., 1 mile; 1 yd., 3 ft.; 16 oz., 1 lb.; 2 pts., 1 qt.

2. Place the stack in the center of the table.

3. Two children can play.

4. The first child draws two cards. If he correctly identifies that the cards match, he keeps the cards. If they do not match, he places them face up in the discard stack.

5. The second child can either pick two cards from the draw stack or pick one ·card from the draw stack and one card from the discard stack to "chance" a match.

6. If a child discards two cards that match, the second player can claim the cards and still takes a turn.

7. The child with the most cards wins the game.

NUMBER CONCEPT CARDS p. 105. Play as a card game (see "Deal the Deck," p. 74). Match numbers and number groups to form sets or books. Reduce visual stimulation by using dots or other geometric symbols rather than pictures. Use with "Reach Your Goal" p. 85.

STEP AND CLAP p. 106. The teacher holds up a card with a number group or number. The child goes to the same stepping card that is indicated on the teacher's card. The teacher can either use flash cards or give arithmetic problems orally. The child steps on the card showing the answer. Make an additional set of stepping cards using colors and color words. Make a set showing different shapes.

DROP A LINE p. 108. Other objects can be drawn or pasted on the paper fish—for example, letters, words, clocks, colors, shapes. The child keeps the fish he identifies.

BUTTON DICE p. 110. For large number recognition, the child says the larger of the two numbers and places the equivalent of the larger number of buttons in the pot.

Addition Button Dice—Thirty buttons are placed in the pot. The child rolls the dice and takes from the pot the number of buttons indicated by the total of the dice.

Subtraction Button Dice—Same as addition, except the child subtracts the smaller number from the larger number and takes from the pot the number of buttons indicated by the remainder. If the child rolls doubles,

MATH BINGO p. 113. Use the basic grid masters to construct bingo games relating to shapes and colors (use gummed paper), letter and word recognition, phonics, and opposites.

MATH DICE p. 120. This can be adapted for multiplication or column adding with the use of additional cubes.

APPENDIX
CROSS-CLASSIFICATION
OF INSTRUCTIONAL ACTIVITIES

Skills and Concepts	Page Numbers
Auditory Discrimination/ Listening	18, 56, 66, 89, 90, 93, 98
Blends	86
Body Image	49
Classification	43, 69, 70, 81, 94, 105
Color Discrimination	20, 34, 35, 37, 40, 42, 52, 66, 69
Concept of Half	41
Counting	24, 38, 40, 89, 105, 106, 107, 112, 117, 118, 123
Directional Concepts	47, 90, 93, 126
Eye-Hand Coordination	23, 25, 26, 27, 28, 29, 30, 31, 32, 33, 34, 35, 36, 37, 38, 39, 44, 49, 118
Figure-Ground Discrimination	43, 53, 55, 74
Following Directions	18, 27, 36, 47, 54, 55, 59, 66, 89, 90, 92, 93, 112
Form Discrimination	20, 34, 35, 37, 40, 52, 66, 69
Gross Motor	28, 57, 58, 59, 106, 121
Initial, Medial, Final Sounds	75, 77, 81, 84, 85
Letter Formation	23

Letter Recognition 18, 19, 22, 23, 45, 54, 67, 68, 76, 79, 80, 81, 82, 84, 85

Matching—Shape, Color, Letter, Word 21, 41, 42, 67, 81, 84, 114, 129

Measurement 125, 129

Number Group Recognition 22, 23, 40, 45, 53, 105, 106, 108, 110, 111, 112, 113, 114, 115, 118, 123

Number Formation 19, 120

Number Recognition 18, 19, 22, 23, 40, 45, 53, 105, 106, 108, 110, 111, 112, 113, 114, 115, 116, 118, 120, 122, 123, 126

Number Sequence 24, 38, 40, 105, 106, 112, 117, 118, 123

Observing Detail 73

Part-Whole 34, 41, 46, 49, 50, 55, 72, 76

Parts of Speech 88, 96, 97

Place Value 127, 128

Position in Space 48, 51, 93

Reading 23, 32, 59, 89

Rhyming 84

Sequencing 30, 54, 72, 78, 80, 91, 96, 97, 107

Shape Recognition 18, 23, 34, 43, 79, 89

Sentence Construction 96, 97

Simple Computation 38, 108, 109, 110, 111, 115, 116, 117, 119, 120, 121, 124

Size Concepts 27

Spatial Relationships 52

Spelling	87, 107
Tactile-Kinesthetic Discrimination	18, 20, 21, 22, 23, 24, 27, 48
Thinking Skills	20, 40, 43, 46, 50, 69, 70, 73, 90, 94, 95, 98
Time Concepts	122, 123
Verbal Expression	20, 21, 26, 45, 48, 49, 70, 71, 72, 73, 82, 85, 94, 95, 98
Visual Discrimination	18, 30, 34, 51, 74, 87
Visual Memory	42, 45, 47, 48, 79
Word Association	71
Word Formation	21
Word Recognition	21, 45, 50, 66, 67, 68, 77, 78, 79, 80, 82, 83, 84, 85, 86, 91, 95